African wildlife

ALPHABET
and
NUMBER

BOOK

African wildlife

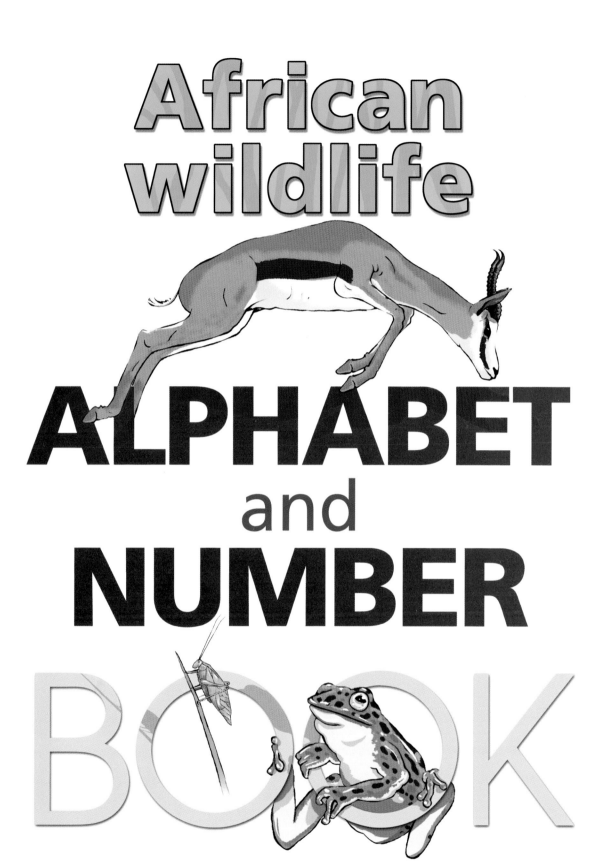

ALPHABET
and
NUMBER

BOOK

Illustrated by DAVID DU PLESSIS

There are twenty-six letters in the alphabet

A B C D E

1 2 3 4 5

K L M N

11 12 13 14

S T U V

19 20 21 22

Aa
is for

albatross

antlion

aloe

anemone

abalone

1 one octopus

acacia

antelope

ant

anthill

aardwolf

aardvark

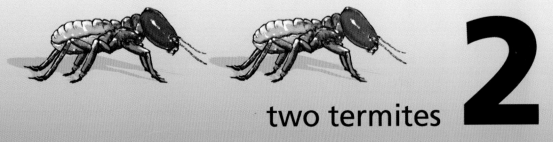

two termites

2

Bb is for

bushbaby

baobab

bontebok

blister beetle

bat

baboon

3 three trees

butterfly

bateleur

bushpig

bee

buffalo

four bullfrogs

4

Cc is for

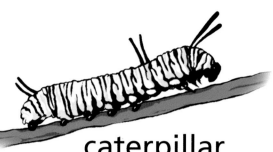
caterpillar

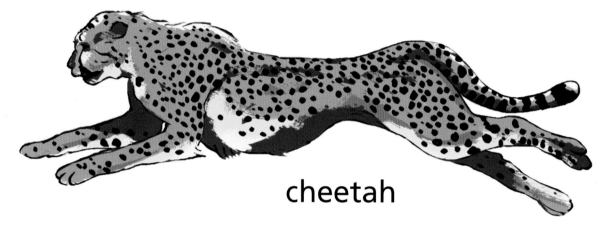
cheetah

cricket

crocodile

crab

5

five fishes

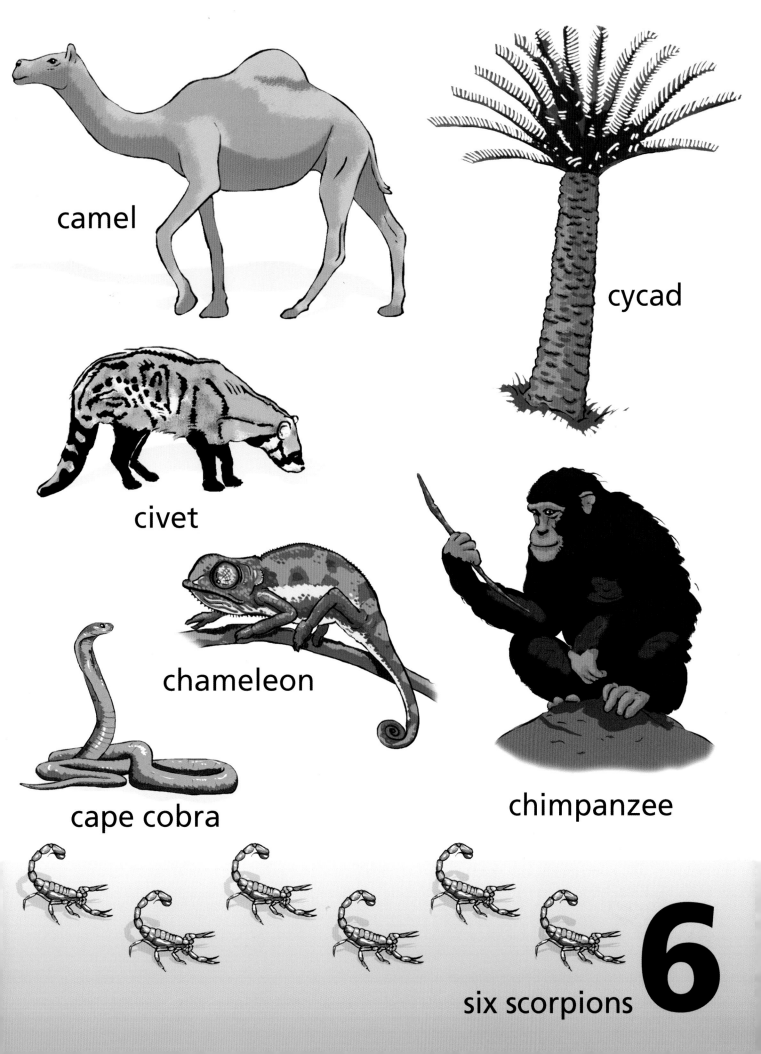

camel

cycad

civet

chameleon

chimpanzee

cape cobra

six scorpions 6

Dd is for

disa

dik-dik

dove

dassie

dung beetle

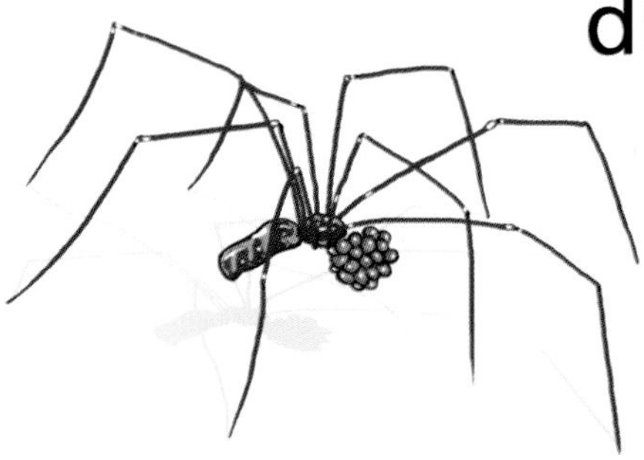

daddy long legs

7 seven snails

dragonfly

duiker

dolphin

dormouse

eight eland

8

Ee **is for**

elephant

egret

erica

earwig

elephant-shrew

9 nine nyala

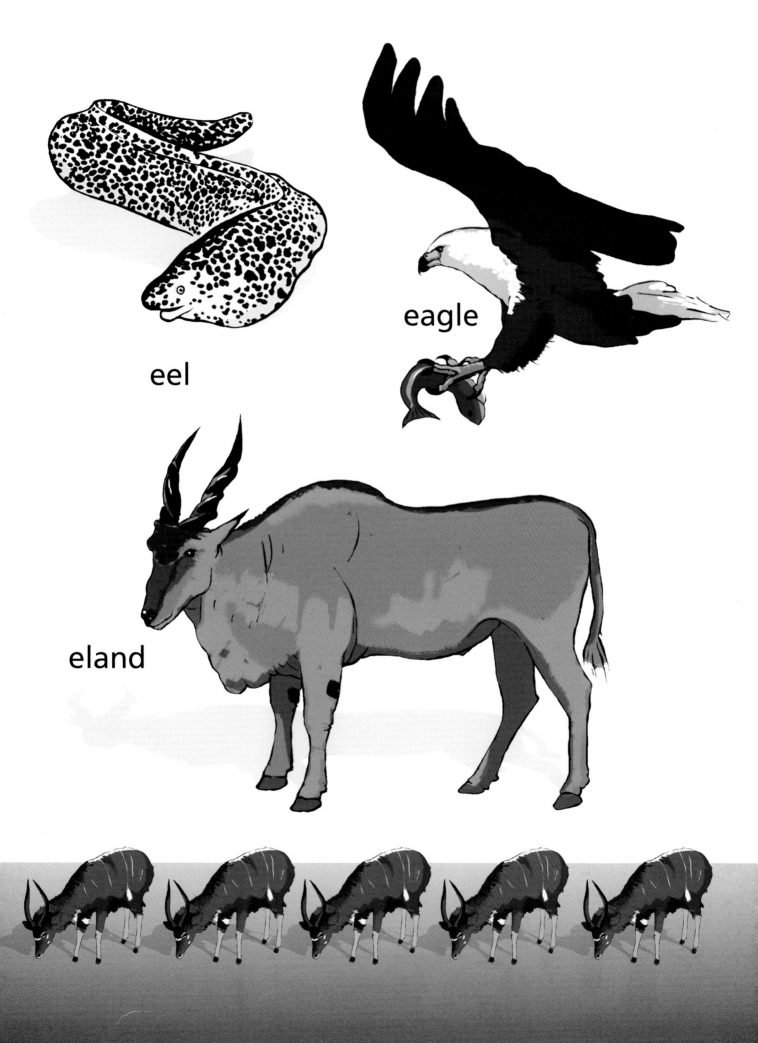

eel

eagle

eland

Ff is for

feather

flamingo

flea

fossil

frog

10 ten tilapia

francolin

fly

fiscal flycatcher

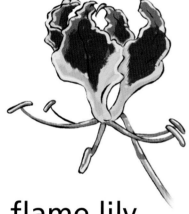

flame lily

fox

firefly

Gg is for

gecko

gorilla

grasshopper

gemsbok

goose

11

eleven egrets

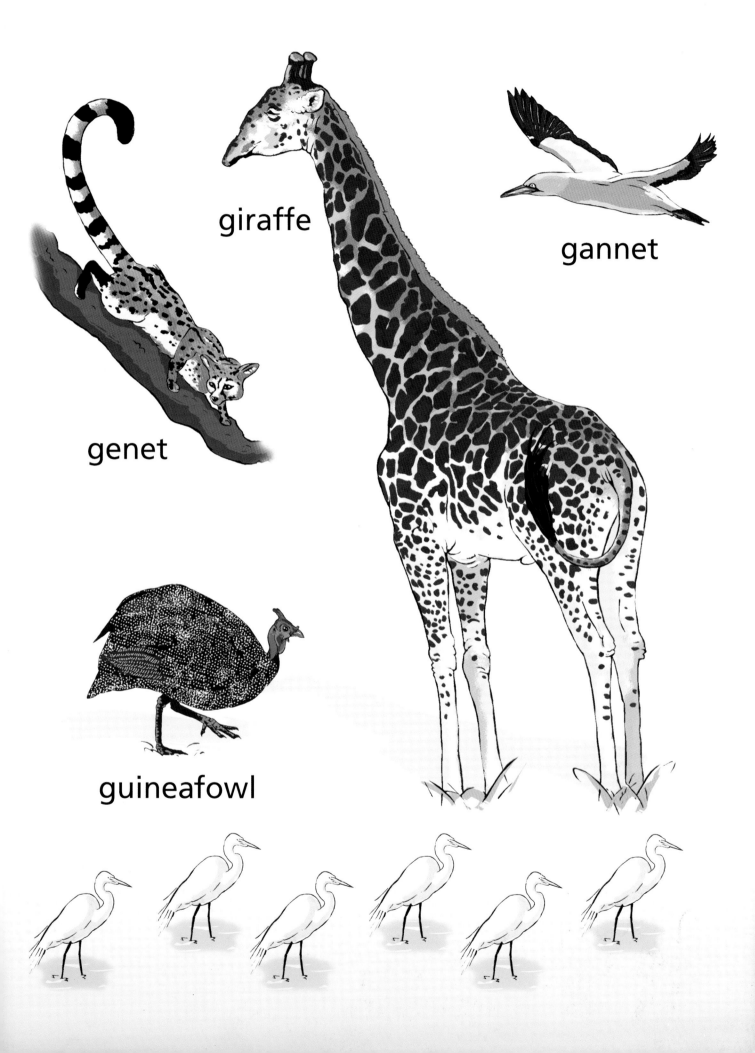

genet

giraffe

gannet

guineafowl

Hh is for

hippopotamus

hornbill

hare

12 twelve tadpoles

hartebeest

hoopoe

honey badger

hyena

hedgehog

Ii is for

impala

iris

ibis

13 thirteen tracks

Jj is for

jellyfish

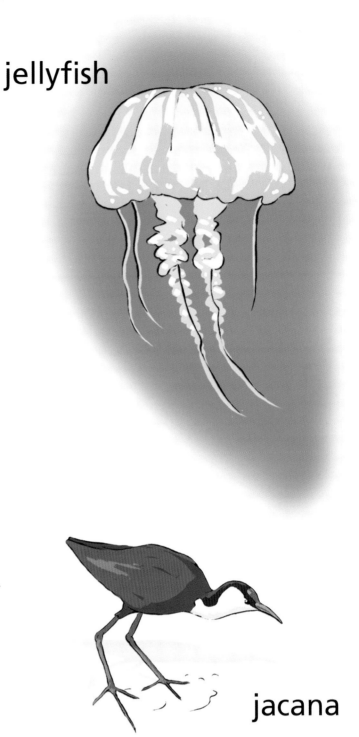

jackal

jacana

Kk
is for

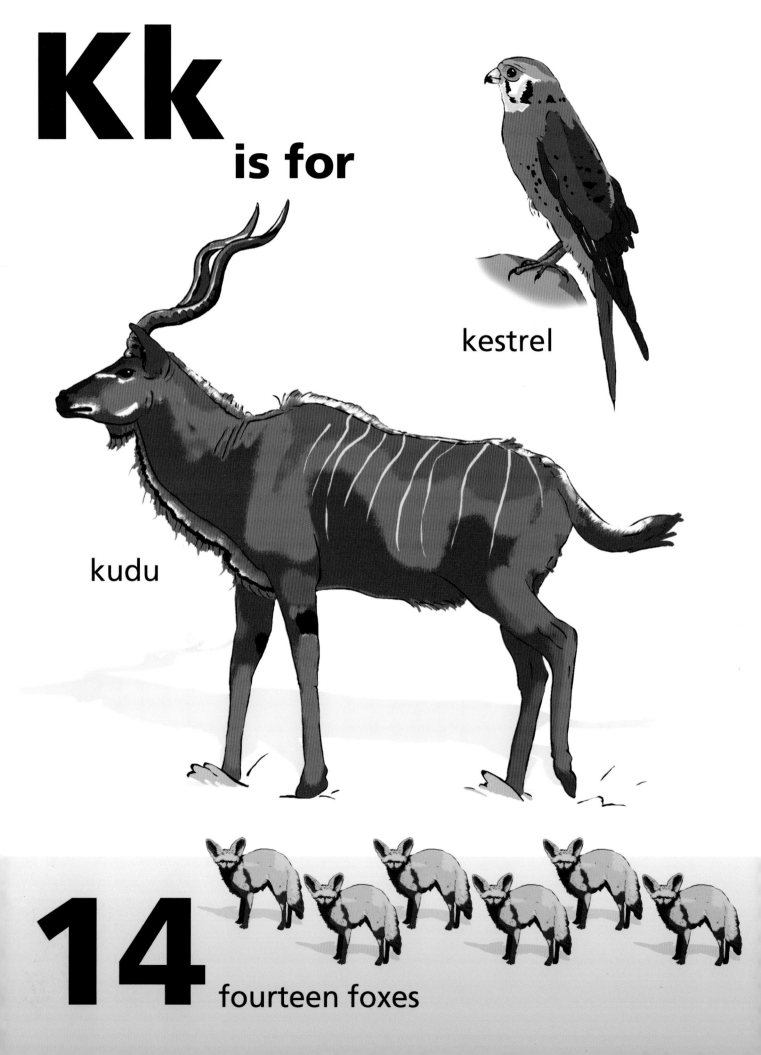

kestrel

kudu

14
fourteen foxes

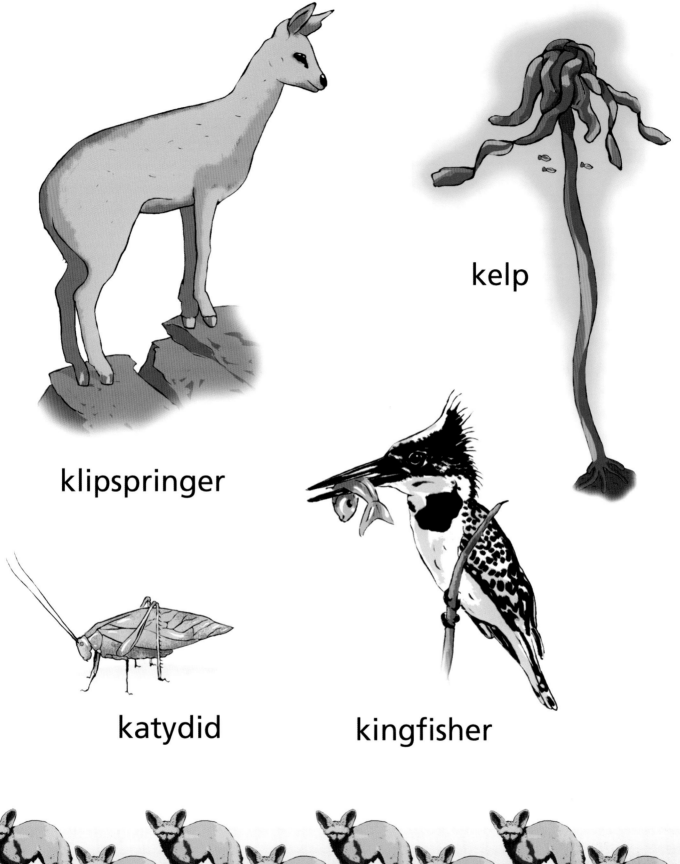

klipspringer

kelp

katydid

kingfisher

Ll is for

lourie

lily

lion

ladybird

15 fifteen francolins

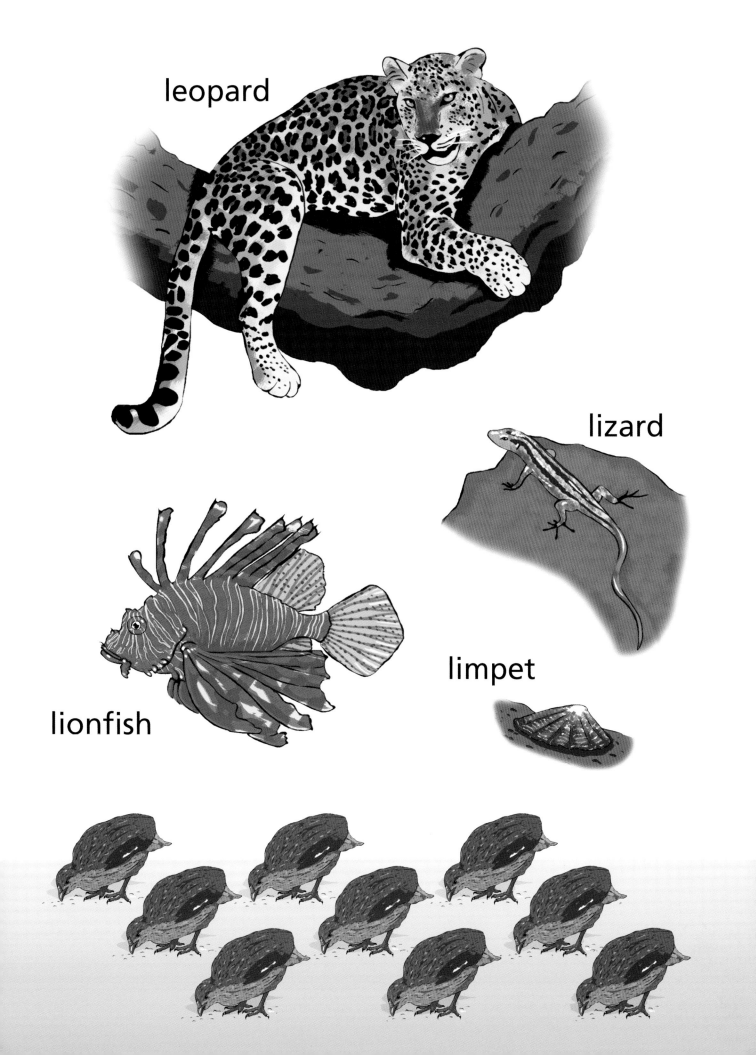

leopard

lizard

lionfish

limpet

Mm is for

mopane worm

mopane tree

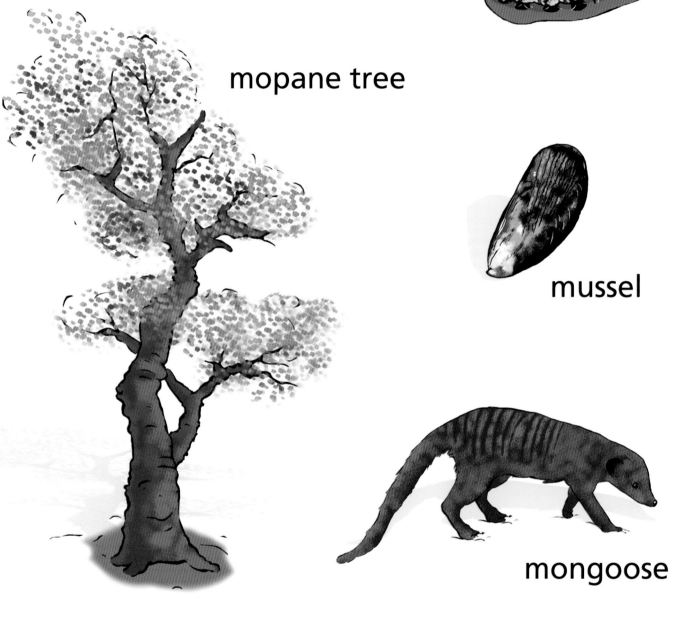

mussel

mongoose

16 sixteen spiders

meerkat

moth

mouse

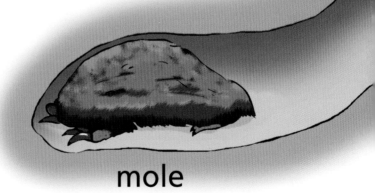

mole

mosquito

Nn
is for

nyala

17
seventeen seals

night sky

Namaqualand daisy

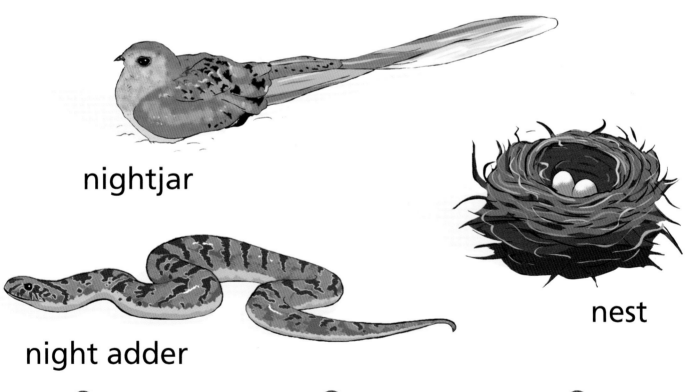

nightjar

nest

night adder

Oo **is for**

owl

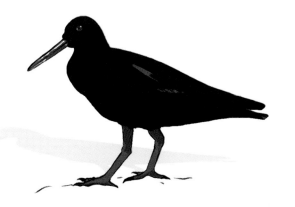

oystercatcher

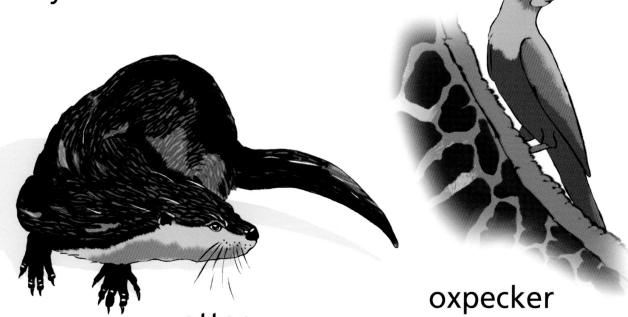

otter

oxpecker

18

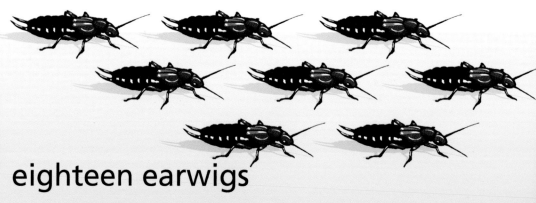

eighteen earwigs

ostrich

octopus

oyster

Pp is for

protea

pangolin

praying mantis

peacock

19

nineteen nests

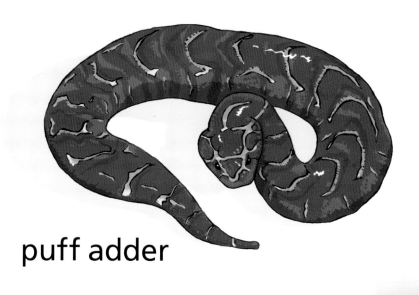

puff adder

pansy shell

prawn

penguin

porcupine

Qq is for

quiver tree

20 twenty trumpeter hornbills

quelea

quail

Rr is for

rock monitor

rhinoceros

red roman

red bishop

21

twenty-one three-banded plovers

reedbuck

red rock rabbit

rat

ray

Ss is for

sunflower

spider

springbok

sunbird

scorpion

22
twenty-two turtles

shark

secretarybird

snail

starfish

seal

Tt is for

tracks

tsessebe

termite

tortoise

three-banded plover

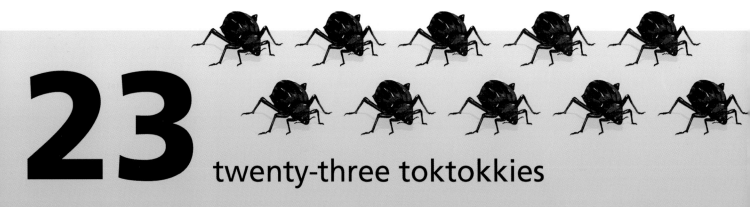

23

twenty-three toktokkies

toktokkie

trumpeter hornbill

turtle

tadpole

tree squirrel

Uu
is for

urchin

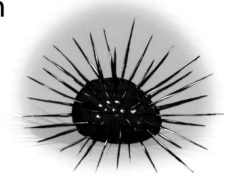

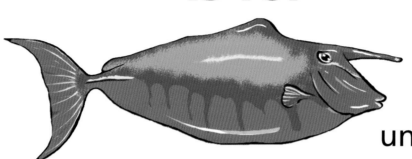

unicorn fish

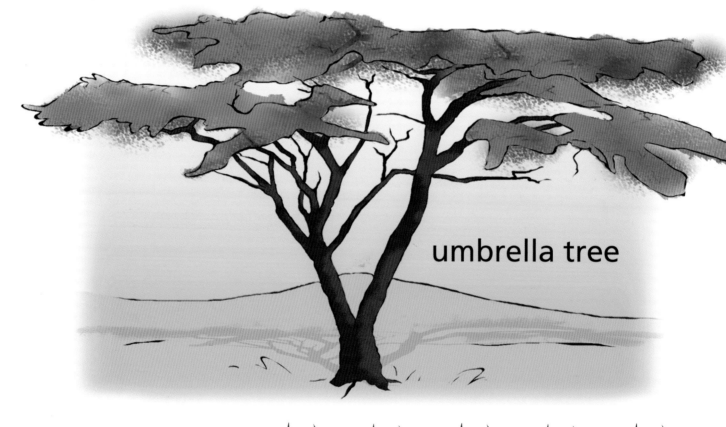

umbrella tree

24
twenty-four tsessebe

Vv is for

velvet ant

vervet monkey

vulture

Ww is for

waxbill

whale

wasp

wildebeest

25 twenty-five tortoises

wild dog

weaver bird

worm

warthog

welwitchia

waterhole

Xx **is for**

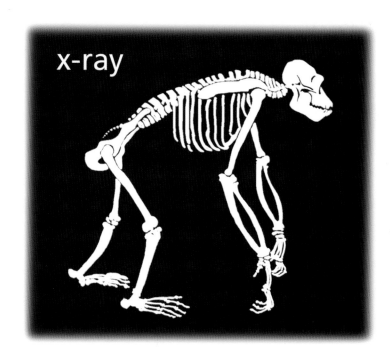

x-ray

Yy **is for**

yellow-billed stork

yellowtail

26

twenty-six tree squirrels

Zz is for

zorilla

zebra

Animal hides

Match the skin type or pattern on the right to the animal on the left.

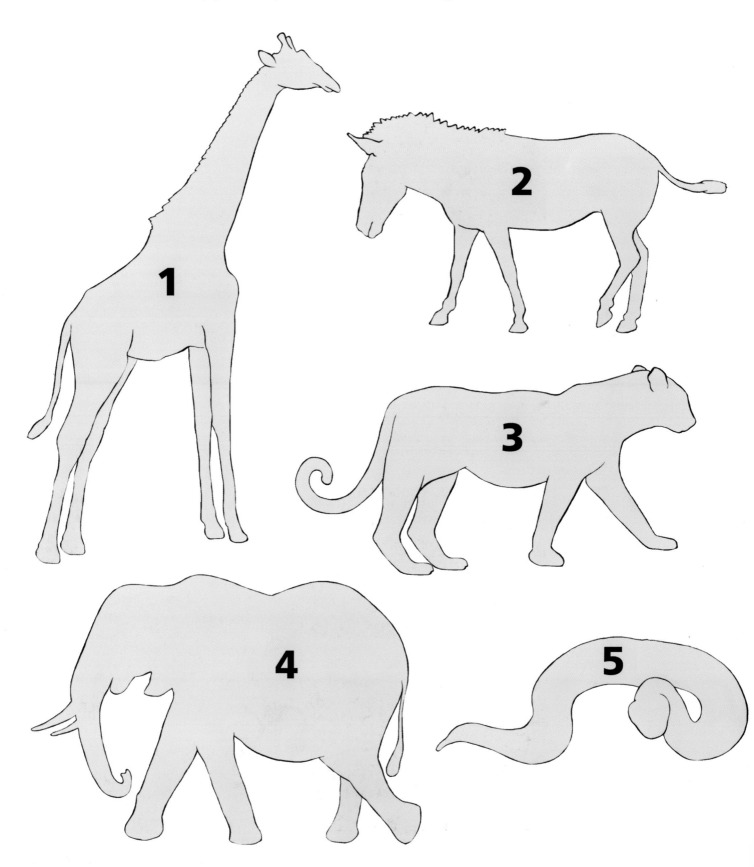

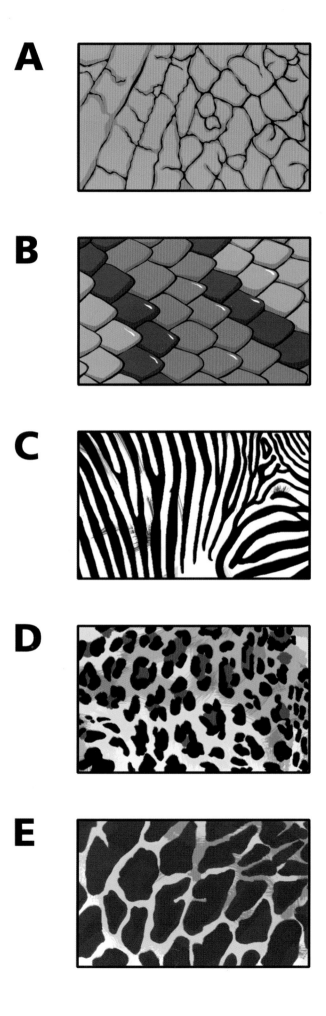

Opposites

fast

slow

fat

thin

light

heavy

hard

soft

tall

short

big

small

Big 5

The elephant, leopard, buffalo, rhinoceros and lion are called the Big 5. These are the animals people most want to see when they visit game reserves.

elephant

The elephant is the biggest land animal in Africa.

rhinoceros

Africa has two types of rhinoceros, the **black rhinoceros** eats leaves and the **white rhinoceros** eats grass.

Little 5

elephant-shrew

buffalo-weaver

leopard

Leopards hunt at night
and stay well hidden in
trees and long grass
in the day time.

buffalo

Buffaloes live in groups
called herds and
have big curved horns.

lion

Lions live in large family groups
called prides. Male lions have
big shaggy manes.

antlion   rhinoceros beetle   leopard tortoise

The bushveld

Many game reserves, such as the Kruger National Park, are in the bushveld. Lots of animals and birds live there.

Along the river

Africa's rivers are full of interesting animals.
Some live in the water and others visit to drink and bath.

Along the seashore

There are lots of curious creatures under the ocean and on the beach. How many can you name?

Night time

Some animals only come out at night to hunt and feed. They rest during the day.

Struik Publishers
(A division of New Holland Publishing (South Africa) (Pty) Ltd)
Cornelis Struik House
80 McKenzie Street
Cape Town
8001

New Holland Publishing is a member of the Johnnic Publishing Group.

www.struik.co.za

**Log on to our photographic website
www.imagesofafrica.co.za for an African experience.**

First published in 2005
1 3 5 7 9 10 8 6 4 2

Publishing manager: Pippa Parker
Managing editor: Lynda Harvey
Concept design: Janice Evans
Illustrator: David du Plessis

Reproduction by Hirt and Carter Cape (Pty) Ltd
Printed and bound by Kyodo Printing Co (S'pore) Pte Ltd, Singapore

ISBN 1 77007 152 0